# —DELECTABLE—
# CHRISTMAS TREATS

*Judi Olstein*

Sweetwater Press
*Florence, Alabama*

Published by Sweetwater Press
P.O. Box 1855
Florence, Alabama 35631

Copyright © 1994 by The Triangle Group, Ltd.
Photographs © 1994 by George G. Wieser
 and © 1993 by Melanie Acevedo

The candy recipes in this book are from *Kris Kringle's Christmas
Candy Cookbook,* Grandma Kate Books, 98-1268 Kaahumanu
Street, Honolulu, Hawaii 96782. Reprinted with permission.

Produced by The Triangle Group, Ltd.
227 Park Avenue
Hoboken, NJ 07030

Design: Tony Meisel
Special thanks to Risa Gary of Mikasa, New York
Origination and printing: Cronion S.A., Barcelona

Printed in Spain

ISBN 1-884822-05-3

# Contents

| | |
|---|---|
| Introduction | 5 |
| Thumbprint Cookies | 7 |
| Snickerdoodles | 9 |
| Peanut Butter Kisses | 11 |
| Rolled Spice Cookies | 13 |
| Sugary Lemon Cut-Outs | 15 |
| Wedding Cakes | 17 |
| Lemon-Nut Biscotti | 19 |
| Crescents | 21 |
| Hermits | 23 |
| Frosted Lemon Butter Balls | 25 |
| Hazelnut Butter Balls | 27 |
| Raspberry Crumb Bars | 29 |
| Almond Macaroons | 31 |
| Pinwheel Cookies | 33 |
| Spritz Cookies | 35 |
| Chocolate-Rum Fruitcake | 37 |
| Wintergreen Mints | 39 |
| Cherry Puffs | 41 |
| Tutti-Frutti Roll | 43 |
| Coconut Drops | 45 |
| Maple Pralines | 47 |
| Five Minute Fudge | 49 |
| Almond Squares | 51 |
| Salt Water Taffy | 53 |
| Caramel Pinwheels | 55 |
| Heavenly Truffles | 57 |
| Butterscotch Drops | 59 |
| Butter Crunch | 61 |

# Introduction

Christmas may come but once a year, but it comes with a vengeance. Shopping, wrapping gifts, setting up the tree, cooking, baking, entertaining—all conspire for much jollity and equal exhaustion.

But what would Christmas be without sweets—cookies, cakes and candies—to celebrate the holiday season? From a simple, festively colored mint to a rich, dark and luscious fruit cake, Christmas treats are a tradition that we all look forward to with greedy glee.

Some of these confections, especially the candies and cookies, can be made as a family adventure, all the more satisfying in the ensuing hilarity and anticipation. Others are complex and time-consuming—especially the fruit cakes—but the results are well worth it.

These are festive sweets, remember, and their production should be considered part of the celebrations. Likewise, the ingredients should be only the best. Fresh butter, flour, the finest essences and fruits and nuts will make for far superior goods and will be far more appreciated.

Almost all the recipes in this book make excellent gifts, especially when prettily and imaginatively wrapped and decorated. Just don't get too carried away. Even the best cookie in the world can become lost in a mound of decorative icings and nut meats. Your Christmas treats should be remembered for the entire year.

# Thumbprint Cookies

1 cup sweet butter, softened
1 cup sugar
2 teaspoons pure vanilla extract
2 eggs, separated
2 1/2 cups flour, sifted
1 cup finely chopped pecans
raspberry or blackberry jam

In a medium-size bowl beat the butter, sugar, vanilla, and egg yolks at a high speed until light and fluffy. Gradually stir in the flour with a wooden spoon. Gather the dough in a ball and wrap in plastic. Refrigerate 4 hours or until firm.

Preheat the oven to 300 degrees F.

Form the dough into balls by using a level teaspoon. Dip the balls into the egg whites and then roll them in the chopped pecans.

Arrange the balls on ungreased baking sheets, approximately 1 inch apart. Using your thumb or the end of a wooden spoon, make an indentation in each cookie. Fill the indentation with the jam.

Bake cookies for 20 minutes or until golden. Remove to cooling racks. Makes approximately 48 cookies.

# Snickerdoodles

1 cup sweet butter, softened
1 1/2 cups plus 2 tablespoons sugar
2 eggs
2 3/4 cups flour
2 teaspoons cream of tartar
1 teaspoon baking soda
1/4 teaspoon salt
2 teaspoons cinnamon

In a large bowl beat the butter until soft, add 1 1/2 cups of the sugar and the eggs and continue beating until light and fluffy.

In another bowl combine the flour, cream of tartar, baking soda and salt. Add this to the first mixture and stir until well blended. Cover the bowl and refrigerate for 1 hour.

Preheat the oven to 375 degrees F. In a small bowl combine the remaining sugar and cinnamon. Shape the dough into balls approximately 2 inches in diameter and roll in the cinnamon sugar. Place the balls 3 inches apart on ungreased baking sheets.

Bake the cookies for 12 to 15 minutes or until golden. Remove to cooling racks when done. Makes approximately 24 large cookies. (Make sure to leave plenty of room between the cookies on the sheet, these cookies will puff up and then flatten out as they bake.)

# Peanut Butter Kisses

2 cups smooth peanut butter
1 1/4 cups sugar
2 eggs
48 milk chocolate kisses

Preheat the oven to 350 degrees F.

In a medium-size bowl combine the peanut butter, sugar and eggs until well blended.

With well-floured hands (the dough will be sticky) form level tablespoons of the dough and roll it into balls. Place balls approximately 2 inches apart on ungreased baking sheets.

Bake the cookies for 12 to 15 minutes or until the tops begin to crack and the cookies are dry to the touch. Remove the sheets from the oven and immediately press a chocolate kiss into the center of each cookie. Allow the cookies to cool on the sheets for 2 minutes before removing to racks to cool. Makes approximately 48 cookies.

# Rolled Spice Cookies

4 cups flour
1 teaspoon ground cinnamon
1 teaspoon ground nutmeg
1/2 teaspoon ground ginger
1/4 teaspoon ground cloves
1/2 teaspoon salt
1 1/2 cups sweet butter, softened
1 cup sugar
1 egg
1 teaspoon pure vanilla extract
Icing:
1 cup sifted confectioners sugar
1/4 teaspoon salt
1/2 teaspoon pure vanilla extract
1 1/2 tablespoons heavy cream
 red or green food coloring

In a large bowl combine the flour, cinnamon, nutmeg, ginger, cloves and salt.

In another large bowl beat the butter and sugar together until light and fluffy. Add the egg and the vanilla extract, beat until blended. With the mixer on the lowest speed, gradually add the flour-spice mixture. Continue mixing until blended.

Separate the dough into 3 equal pieces, flatten each piece and wrap in plastic wrap. Refrigerate until firm, about 1 hour.

Preheat the oven to 375 degrees F. Remove dough from the refrigerator. On a lightly floured surface, roll the dough, one piece at a time, to 1/4-inch thickness. Using floured cookie cutters, cut into desired shapes.

Place the cookies 1 inch apart on ungreased baking sheets and bake for 10-12 minutes or until the edges are just brown. Transfer cookies to racks to cool. Continue re-rolling the scraps until all the dough has been used. After cookies are cool decorate with icing.

## Icing

In a small bowl combine the sugar, salt and vanilla extract. Add the cream and stir until blended. Add desired food coloring, stir to blend. Apply to cooled cookies with a spatula or pastry tube. Allow the icing to dry. Makes approximately 48 cookies.

# Sugary Lemon Cut-Outs

1 cup sweet butter, softened
3/4 cup sugar
1/2 teaspoon salt
1 egg
1 egg yolk
2 tablespoons fresh lemon juice
1 teaspoon pure vanilla or almond extract
4 cups flour
white, red and green sugar for decorating

Combine the butter, 3/4 cup sugar and salt together in a large bowl, beat until light and fluffy. Add the egg, the egg yolk, lemon juice and vanilla extract, beat until blended. With the mixer on the lowest speed, gradually add the flour, beat until just mixed.

Form the dough into a large ball and then separate into 2 equal pieces. Wrap each half in plastic and refrigerate for 4 hours or until firm.

Preheat the oven to 350 degrees F. Grease baking sheets with butter.

Remove the dough from the refrigerator. On a lightly floured surface, roll the dough, one piece at a time, to approximately 1/8-inch thickness. Cut with desired Christmas cookie cutters. Place each cookie on the sheets, approximately 1 inch apart. Sprinkle cookies with white, red or green sugar.

Bake for 10-12 minutes or until the edges are just light brown. Remove from the oven and transfer cookies to racks to cool. Makes approximately 68 cookies.

# Wedding Cakes

1 cup sweet butter, softened
1/2 cup confectioners sugar
1 teaspoon pure vanilla extract
1/4 teaspoon salt
2 cups flour
confectioners sugar

In a large bowl, cream the butter until light and fluffy. Add the sugar, vanilla extract and salt. Beat until well blended. Add the flour and stir until well mixed. Cover the bowl and refrigerate for 30 minutes or until dough is firm enough to handle.

Preheat the oven to 375 degrees F.

Remove the dough from the refrigerator and shape into 1-inch balls. Space 1 inch apart on ungreased baking sheets. Bake for 12-15 minutes or until light golden in color.

Remove from the oven and transfer cookies to cooling racks. Place the cookies close together. While cookies are still warm, dust heavily with confectioners sugar. Cool completely. Makes approximately 48 cookies.

# Lemon-Nut Biscotti

3 1/2 cups flour
1 tablespoon baking powder
1/2 cup low-fat margarine, softened
3/4 cup sugar
5 eggs
2 tablespoons freshly grated lemon peel
1 cup pine nuts
3/4 cup shelled pistachio nuts
1 egg white, lightly beaten
sugar for sprinkling

In a large bowl, or on a sheet of waxed paper, combine the flour and baking powder.

In a large bowl combine the margarine and sugar and beat until fluffy and light in color. Add the eggs, lemon peel and vanilla and beat until the mixture is smooth and thick.

Add the flour gradually and mix well after each addition. Add the nuts and stir.

Gather the dough into a ball and divide it into 3 equal parts. Wrap each part in plastic wrap and refrigerate for 5 hours or until easy to handle.

Preheat the oven to 350 degrees F. Spray baking sheets with a low-calorie cooking spray.

Remove the dough from the refrigerator and transfer each section to a lightly floured surface. Shape each portion into a large log. Place 2 of the logs on 1 sheet about 4-5 inches apart, place the remaining log on the other sheet. Brush each log with the egg white and sprinkle with the sugar.

Bake for 30 to 35 minutes or until the dough has flattened somewhat and the top is slightly cracked.

Remove the sheets from the oven. Using a large metal spatula, loosen the dough from the sheet and allow it to cool for 8 to 10 minutes. Carefully transfer the logs, one at a time, to a cutting board.

With a large knife, slice each log into diagonal slices. Return to the baking sheets only after they have been wiped clean. The slices may be placed close together. Bake for 10 to 15 minutes, turning twice, until the biscotti are dry and lightly toasted. Remove from oven and cool on racks. Makes approximately 40 biscotti.

# Crescents

1 cup sweet butter, softened
1/2 cup confectioners sugar
2 teaspoons pure vanilla extract
1/4 teaspoon salt
1 3/4 cups flour
1 cup finely ground walnuts
1/2 cup sugar

In a large bowl cream together the butter, confectioners sugar, vanilla extract and salt until light and fluffy. Add the flour and walnuts and stir until well blended. Cover the bowl and chill until the dough is firm enough to handle, approximately 45 minutes.

Preheat the oven to 300 degrees F.

Remove the dough from the refrigerator. Working on a lightly floured board, break off small pieces of dough and roll into finger-thick strips. Cut the strips into 2-inch lengths. Taper the ends and shape into crescents.

Place the cookies 1 inch apart on ungreased baking sheets. Bake for 18-20 minutes or until cookies are firm.

Remove from the oven. While the cookies are still warm roll them in the sugar. Be careful not to remove them from the sheets too quickly or they may crumble. Cool on wire racks. Makes approximately 60 cookies.

# Hermits

1/2 cup sugar
1/3 cup sweet butter, softened
1 egg
3 cups flour
1/2 teaspoon salt
1 teaspoon cinnamon
1/2 teaspoon grated nutmeg
1/2 cup molasses
1/2 cup buttermilk
1 cup raisins

Preheat the oven to 350 degrees F. Grease baking sheets with butter and set aside.

In a mixing bowl cream together the sugar and butter until light and fluffy. Beat in the egg.

Combine the flour, salt, cinnamon and nutmeg together in a bowl. In a measuring cup, combine the molasses with the buttermilk. Add the molasses mixture alternately with the flour to the creamed sugar and butter. Stir in the raisins.

Drop the dough by teaspoonfuls approximately 1 inch apart on the baking sheets. Bake for 8-10 minutes or until lightly browned. Cool on wire rack. Makes approximately 72 cookies.

# Frosted Lemon Butter Balls

1 cup sweet butter, softened
1/2 cup confectioners sugar
1 1/2 cups flour
3/4 cup cornstarch
1/4 teaspoon salt
2 teaspoons grated lemon rind
1 cup finely chopped blanched almonds

Frosting
1 cup confectioners sugar
2 tablespoons sweet butter, melted
1 tablespoon lemon juice

Preheat the oven to 350 degrees F. Lightly grease baking sheets and set aside.

In a large bowl cream together the butter and sugar until light and fluffy.

Sift the flour, cornstarch and salt together onto a piece of waxed paper. Add to the butter mixture, mix well. Add the lemon rind and stir.

Shape the dough into 1-inch balls and roll in the chopped almonds. Press nuts in gently. Place cookies 1 inch apart on baking sheets. Bake for 15 minutes. Remove from the oven and transfer to wire racks to cool.

To make the frosting, in a small bowl combine the confectioners sugar, melted butter and lemon juice. Stir until smooth. Drizzle frosting over cooled cookies. Allow frosting to harden before storing cookies. Makes approximately 40 cookies.

# Hazelnut Butter Balls

1/2 cup sweet butter, softened
1/4 cup sugar
1 egg, separated
1 tablespoon white rum
1/2 teaspoon pure vanilla extract
1 cup flour
1/2 cup finely chopped hazelnuts

In a medium-size bowl, cream together the butter and sugar until light and fluffy. Add the egg yolk, white rum and vanilla extract. Beat until well blended. Add the flour and mix well. Cover the bowl and refrigerate 4 hours or overnight.

Preheat oven to 325 degrees F. Lightly grease baking sheets.

Remove the dough from the refrigerator. Form the dough into 3/4-inch balls. Place the chopped hazelnuts in one bowl, and the egg white in another bowl. Lightly beat the egg white.

Dip the top of each ball into the egg white and then into the hazelnuts. Place cookies, nut side up, 1 inch apart on a baking sheets. Bake for 12-15 minutes or until golden brown.

Remove from the oven and transfer to racks for cooling. Makes approximately 42 cookies.

# Raspberry Crumb Bars

1 3/4 cups flour
1/2 teaspoon baking soda
1 cup sweet butter, softened
1 cup firmly packed light brown sugar
1 1/2 cups quick-cooking rolled oats (not instant)
1 cup raspberry jam

Preheat the oven to 400 degrees F. With butter, grease a
13 x 9 x 2-inch baking pan. Set aside.

In a small bowl combine the flour and the baking
soda. Set aside.

In a medium-size bowl cream together the butter
and the brown sugar until fluffy and light in color. Add the
flour mixture and stir until well blended. Add the oats and
mix well. This may be easiest to do with your hands.

Press half the dough into the prepared pan. Spread
the layer evenly with the jam. Crumble the remaining
dough over the top. Pat gently.

Bake for 20 to 25 minutes or until lightly browned.
Remove from the oven and cool in the pan on a wire rack.
Cut into bars while still warm. Serve warm or cool. Makes
approximately 30 bars.

# Almond Macaroons

1 1/4 cups slivered blanched almonds
3/4 cup sugar
3 egg whites
1/4 teaspoon ground nutmeg
candied cherries or extra slivered blanched almonds

In a food processor or blender grind the nuts until they are very fine.

In a medium-size saucepan, combine the nuts, sugar and egg whites. Cook over a medium heat, stirring constantly for 10 minutes or until the mixture begins to thicken and holds its shape when pressed with a wooden spoon. Remove from the heat and add the nutmeg.

Drop the mixture by level tablespoons onto baking sheets that have been buttered and lightly floured. Allow the macaroons to stand at room temperature until they have cooled.

Preheat the oven to 300 degrees F. Carefully place halves of the candied cherries or slivers of the almonds on the top of the macaroons. Bake for 20 minutes or until just lightly golden. Remove from the baking sheets immediately with a wide spatula. Makes approximately 24 macaroons.

# Pinwheel Cookies

1/2 cup sweet butter, softened
1/4 cup solid vegetable shortening
3/4 cup sugar
2 eggs
2 1/2 cups flour
1 teaspoon baking powder
1 teaspoon salt
2 ounces unsweetened chocolate, melted and cooled

In a large bowl combine the butter, shortening, sugar, eggs and vanilla, beat until well mixed.

In a small bowl combine the flour, baking powder and salt. Stir into the butter mixture and continue stirring until blended.

Carefully divide the dough in half and remove one half from the bowl and wrap it in plastic. To the half remaining in the bowl, add the melted chocolate and stir to mix. Cover and refrigerate both halves for 2 hours or until firm enough to roll.

On a lightly floured board roll the vanilla dough into a rectangle approximately 12 x 9 inches. Roll the chocolate dough to the same dimensions, carefully place the chocolate dough on top of the vanilla dough. Roll the layers of dough together, beginning at the wide end; roll up tightly. Cover with plastic wrap and chill overnight.

Preheat oven to 400 degrees F.

Cut the dough into slices that are 1/8 inch thick and place on ungreased baking sheets. Bake for 8-10 minutes or until just lightly brown. Remove to racks and cool. Makes approximately 72 cookies.

# Spritz Cookies

1 cup sweet butter, softened
1 cup sugar
2 egg yolks
1 teaspoon pure almond extract
2 1/2 cups flour
colored sugars, nut pieces or glazed fruit
    if desired for decoration

Preheat the oven to 350 degrees F.

In a large bowl cream the butter and sugar together until light and fluffy. Beat in the yolks. When the yolks are well blended, add the almond extract. Sift the flour into the mixture, a little at a time. Beat well after each addition.

Place the dough into a cookie press fitted with any shape. Press the shapes out 1 inch apart onto ungreased baking sheets. These cookies can be decorated at this point with colored sugar, nut pieces or bits of glazed fruit.

Bake for 10 minutes or until lightly browned.

Remove from the oven and transfer to wire racks. Makes approximately 48 cookies.

# Chocolate-Rum Fruitcake

2 cups coarsely chopped pecans
1 cup coarsely chopped dates
1 cup raisins
2/3 cup dark rum
2 cups flour
1 tablespoon cinnamon
1 teaspoon salt
1 cup sweet butter, softened
1 1/3 cups sugar
3 ounces semisweet chocolate, melted and cooled
4 large eggs
1 1/2 teaspoons pure vanilla extract
1 cup semisweet chocolate pieces

Topping
3 tablespoons sweet butter, softened
1 cup confectioners sugar
3 tablespoons dark rum

In a large bowl combine the pecans, dates, raisins and rum. Mix well. Cover the bowl and marinate 6 hours or overnight.

Preheat the oven to 300 degrees F. Butter 2 8-inch round pans. Line the pans with foil and butter again.

Into a bowl sift the flour, cinnamon and salt together.

In a large bowl cream together the butter and sugar until light and fluffy. Add the melted chocolate and mix well. Add the eggs, one at a time, beating well after each addition. Scrape down the sides of the bowl with a rubber spatula when necessary. Blend in the vanilla extract.

Add the flour mixture and beat until just combined. Add the marinated fruit and nut mixture and the chocolate pieces. Mix well.

Turn the batter into the prepared pans; divide evenly. Bake for 1 hour and 10 minutes or until a cake tester inserted into the center comes out clean. Remove from the oven. Cool in the pans for 20 minutes. Turn cakes out onto racks and remove the foil. Serve warm or at room temperature.

While cakes cool, prepare the topping. In a bowl cream the butter until soft. Gradually beat in the sugar. Stir in the rum. Cover the bowl and chill topping until firm. Serve cake with topping. Makes 2 8-inch cakes.

# Wintergreen Mints

In a double boiler, combine 2 cups sifted confectioners sugar, 6 1/2 teaspoons water and 1/4 teaspoon wintergreen extract. Add red or green food coloring to desired hue. Cook until it loses its gloss and becomes dull. Immediately drop by teaspoonfuls onto waxed paper or press into candy mold. Makes about 2 dozen.

# Cherry Puffs

2 1/2 cups sugar
1/2 cup water
2 egg whites
2/3 cup light corn syrup
1/4 teaspoon salt
1/2 teaspoon vanilla
1 cup candied cherries

Slice the candied cherries as desired. In a saucepan, cook the sugar, syrup, salt and water, stirring until the sugar is completely dissolved. Continue cooking without stirring until hard ball stage is reached. If any sugar crystals form on the sides of the pan, wash them away with a piece of wet cheesecloth wrapped around the tines of a fork.

Remove from heat and gradually pour the syrup over the egg whites, which have been beaten stiff during the latter part of the cooking of the syrup. Beat during this addition. Continue beating until the candy will hold its shape when dropped from a spoon. Add vanilla and cherries and mix thoroughly. Drop by teaspoonfuls on waxed paper or turn into a slightly greased pan. This candy is attractive when colored a delightful pink.
Makes 1 1/3 pounds.

# Tutti-Frutti Roll

1 cup fine graham cracker crumbs
1/2 cup finely chopped candied cherries
1/4 cup finely chopped candied pineapple
1/2 cup finely chopped marshmallows
1/4 cup finely chopped green maraschino cherries
1/4 cup chopped pecans
1/4 teaspoon nutmeg
1/2 teaspoon cinnamon
1 teaspoon vanilla extract
1/4 cup light cream

Mix all ingredients then shape into 2 rolls, 1 1/2-inch
in diameter. Roll candy in 1/2 cup fine graham cracker
crumbs. Chill overnight. Cut into thin slices.

# Coconut Drops

2 cups sugar
1/2 cup milk
1 1/2 cups shredded coconut
1/2 teaspoon vanilla

Heat sugar and milk over low heat, stirring constantly until sugar is dissolved. Increase heat and cook, stirring constantly, until candy reaches a soft ball stage (when a spoonful of the mixture dropped in cold water can be rolled into a soft ball). Remove from heat. Stir in coconut and vanilla. Drop from teaspoon onto a greased baking sheet. Makes 2 pounds.

# Maple Pralines

2 cups pecans
2 cups light brown sugar
1 cup maple flavored syrup
1/3 cup evaporated milk or cream

Chop the pecans coarsely. Mix the sugar, syrup and evaporated milk or cream. Heat over low heat, stirring constantly until sugar is dissolved. To remove sugar crystals wipe with a dampened piece of cheesecloth wrapped around tines of a fork. Bring mixture to a boil. Cook without stirring to soft ball stage. Remove from heat. Let stand 5 minutes. Add nuts. Stir until syrup is slightly thick and beginning to appear cloudy. Drop from the tip of a teaspoon onto a greased baking sheet or onto waxed paper, forming patties 2 inches in diameter. Cool. Remove and store in airtight container. Makes 1 1/2 pounds.

# Five Minute Fudge

1 2/3 cups granulated sugar
2 tablespoons butter or margarine
1/2 teaspoon salt
2/3 cup undiluted evaporated milk
1 3/4 packages semisweet chocolate pieces
1/2 pound marshmallows, diced
3/4 cup chopped walnuts
1 teaspoon vanilla extract

Grease 9 x 8 x 2-inch pan. In 2 quart saucepan, combine
sugar, margarine, salt and milk. Bring to a boil over
medium heat. Boil five minutes, stirring constantly.
Remove from heat. Add chocolate, marshmallows, walnuts and vanilla extract. Beat vigorously until marshmallows melt. Pour into pan, sprinkle with more nuts if
desired. Cool. Cut into small squares. Makes about
5 dozen.

# Almond Squares

2 cups blanched almonds
2 cups sifted confectioners sugar
rind of 1/2 lemon
2 egg whites

Grind almonds very fine through a food grinder. Be sure the nuts are dry, otherwise you're in for trouble. If they seem moist and oily, spread them over a shallow pan and dry them in a slow oven before grinding. Now put the ground almonds in a large mixing bowl, stir in sugar and lemon rind. Pound hard with the handle of a wooden spoon. Pound about 5 to 7 minutes to get all the flavor mixed through. Add unbeaten egg whites and blend the mixture. Place in a square pan and refrigerate.

# Salt Water Taffy

8 cups sugar
1 cup light corn syrup
1 cup water
1 1/2 teaspoon salt
2 teaspoons glycerin
1 tablespoon butter
2 teaspoons vanilla

In a saucepan, cook all ingredients except butter and vanilla. Stir until sugar is dissolved. If sugar crystals form on the sides of the saucepan during cooking, wash them away with a piece of wet cheesecloth wrapped around the tines of a fork. Continue cooking until the temperature of 260 degrees F. is reached. Remove from stove. Add butter. When butter is melted, pour into a greased pan. When cool enough to handle, gather into a ball and pull until it is rather firm. Add flavoring while pulling. Stretch out in a long rope and cut into pieces of desired size. Usually the pieces of salt water taffy are about 2 inches in length. Wrap in waxed paper or plastic wrap.

Salt Water Taffy can be colored during the pulling. Add coloring to the taffy and pull it through. Color should suit the flavor: wintergreen taffy is usually colored pink; vanilla with white; spearmint with green; cinnamon with red.

# Caramel Pinwheels

1 cup sugar
1/3 cup light corn syrup
1 1/2 cups heavy cream
1 teaspoon vanilla
1/2 lb. fondant

Grease a 1-inch-deep oblong pan. Mix sugar, syrup and 1/2 cup cream in a saucepan. Cook over low heat, stirring constantly, until sugar dissolves. Increase heat and bring mixture to a boil. Cook gently, stirring constantly, until candy thermometer registers 234 degrees F., or when a little of the mixture dropped in cold water forms a soft ball.

Add 1/2 cup cream and cook again to a soft ball stage or 234 degrees F., stirring constantly, then add the last 1/2 cup cream and cook, stirring constantly, until thermometer registers 246 degrees F., or mixture forms a hard ball.

Immediately cool by setting pan in cold water. With as little stirring as possible, mix in vanilla. Pour candy into buttered pan. Cool. When caramel is cool but still pliable, cut in half to form two pieces. Place rolls of fondant on the caramel and roll up like a jelly roll. Chill until firm. Cut into 1/4-inch slices. Makes two 1-pound rolls.

## Fondant
4 cups sugar
1/8 teaspoon cream of tartar
2 cups thin cream
2 teaspoons light corn syrup

Blend sugar and cream of tartar in a large, heavy saucepan. Gradually blend in cream and corn syrup. Place over low heat. Stir until sugar is dissolved and mixture is boiling gently. Cover. Cook for 3 minutes. Remove cover. If crystals form a ring during the cooking process, remove with a damp cloth wrapped around the tines of a fork. Cook without stirring to a firm ball stage. Pour candy mixture at once into a large, cold-water-rinsed platter. Cool candy to lukewarm without disturbing it. Beat with wooden spoon or spatula. Candy will begin to harden gradually. At this stage, roll into long thin cylinders and let firm.

# Heavenly Truffles

2 packages semisweet chocolate pieces
3/4 cup sweetened condensed milk
pinch of salt
1 cup chopped walnuts or 1 cup chopped candied fruit
    or raisins (optional)
1 teaspoon vanilla extract or 1 tablespoon rum

In double boiler, melt chocolate over hot (not boiling) water. Stir in condensed milk, salt, chopped nuts and extract. Pour into waxed paper lined 9x5x3-inch loaf pan. Cool for a few hours. When firm cut into squares. Makes 1 1/4 pound.

# Butterscotch Drops

1/2 cup granulated sugar
1/4 cup white corn syrup
1/4 cup water
1 tablespoon butter or margarine
1/2 teaspoon vanilla extract

In a 2-quart saucepan, combine sugar, corn syrup and water (if using candy thermometer set in place). Cook over low heat, stirring, to 265 degrees F., or until a little mixture in cold water forms a very hard ball. Add butter. Cook to 290 degrees F., or until a little mixture in cold water becomes brittle. Remove from heat. Add vanilla. Drop from teaspoon onto greased cookie sheet. When firm remove with spatula. Makes 2 dozen.